Set in Joe Regular by
Ann Obringer of BTD in NYC

SAGITTARIUS: Ever try fishing with a bow and arrow? This union will have about as much success.

CAPRICORN: The Goat would rather climb every mountain than deal with *your* weepy moods.

AQUARIUS: You want to feast on love, but Aquarius is permanently out to lunch.

PISCES: Two Fish swam in opposite directions. And missed each other.

water for one weepy whiner who wants to be loved all the time. And you are not it.

LEO: Although they prefer meat, Lions will gladly eat Fish if it is properly cooked.

VIRGO: You would actually be happier with a *shark* in your pond. (And so, for that matter, would a shark.)

LIBRA: You love. Libra loves. Libra loves someone else. You cry.

SCORPIO: The Scorpion only has to lose its temper once. Then you can kiss your fins good-bye.

COMPATIBILITY GUIDE
PISCES AND ...

ARIES: Aries would just as soon spear you as eat you.

TAURUS: Strong-minded Taurus will take a long, hard look at your chronic indecision. And then squash you.

GEMINI: The two of you are like intersecting streets that never meet.

CANCER: There's only room in Cancer's pool of

PISCES AT A GLANCE

Motto: Weep and the world weeps with you
Ruling planet: Neptune
Element: Water
Quality: Fishy
First desire: Weep
Last desire: Sob
Secret desire: Keep weeping and sobbing
Animals: Weeping fishes
Key words: Oh, no!

PISCES the FISH

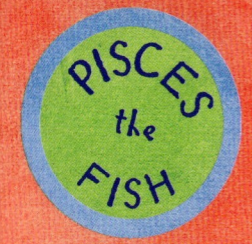

FEBRUARY 20–MARCH 20
Soggy Fish

Yes, you are sweet, kind, adorable, loving, generous, and all that, but you know what? You're also a pain! Indecisive, dreamy, ultra, ultrasensitive, far too delicate for the rough-and-tumble world. Your response to anything unpleasant is to weep. Boo hoo! Put a sock in it, will you? Go swim in a pond.

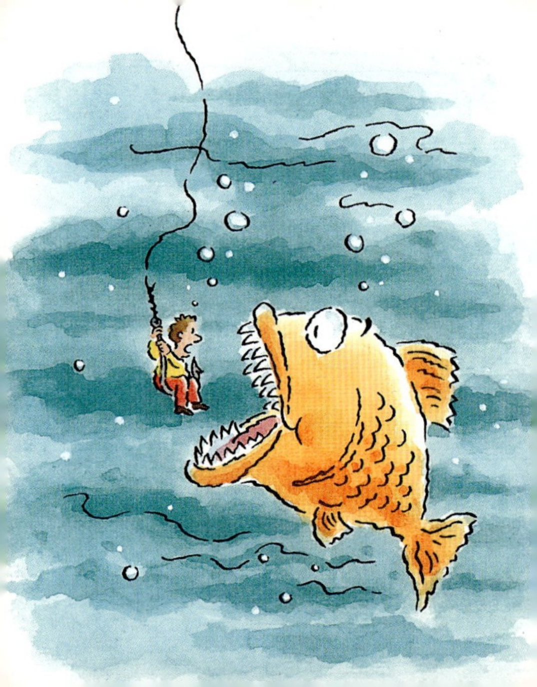

SAGITTARIUS: Twits that pass in the night . . .

CAPRICORN: Goat climbed up the hill to fetch a pail of water. Water Bearer said, "Not now," which led the Goat to slaughter.

AQUARIUS: Zero times zero equals zero.

PISCES: Pisces wants only to be loved, but Aquarius just finds love so *bourgeois*, man.

nose too hard. You would scarcely stir if your house blew up.

LEO: Lions demand constant adoration, but you would be wondering, like, what's the *point*?

VIRGO: You are one of the few who can deal with the Virgin's incessant complaints, because you'll be asleep the entire time.

LIBRA: Way cool. Now you can go back to bed.

SCORPIO: The Scorpion's tail is the dart. And groovy, clueless Aquarius is the board.

COMPATIBILITY GUIDE
AQUARIUS AND...

ARIES: Aries makes war and you make love. These two don't *really* go together very well.

TAURUS: The Bull may dig some grooves in your forehead with its hooves, but that's about it.

GEMINI: You will think about *maybe* showing up for dinner the way the Twins will think about *maybe* inviting you, so *probably* this won't happen.

CANCER: The Crab gets upset if it blows its

AQUARIUS AT A GLANCE

Motto: Like, groovy!
Ruling planet: All of them
Element: Airhead
Quality: Way laid-back
First desire: Mellow out
Last desire: Chill
Secret desire: Save some forests and stuff
Animals: Anything peaceful and groovy
Key words: Like, wow man!

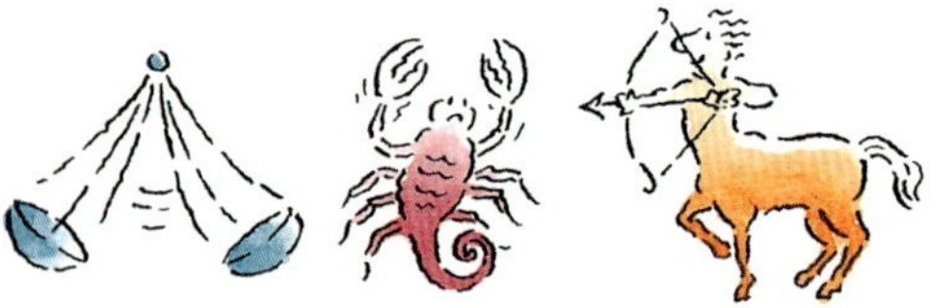

AQUARIUS the WATER BEARER

JANUARY 21–FEBRUARY 19
Clueless in the Aquarium

Far out, man. Mellow. Remember the word "groovy"? You're it. You are the embodiment of everything beaded, sandaled, and psychedelic.

You care, man. You feel a lot of love. You want to make the planet a better place—as soon as you figure out which planet you're from. Here's a piece of advice:

Get a life!

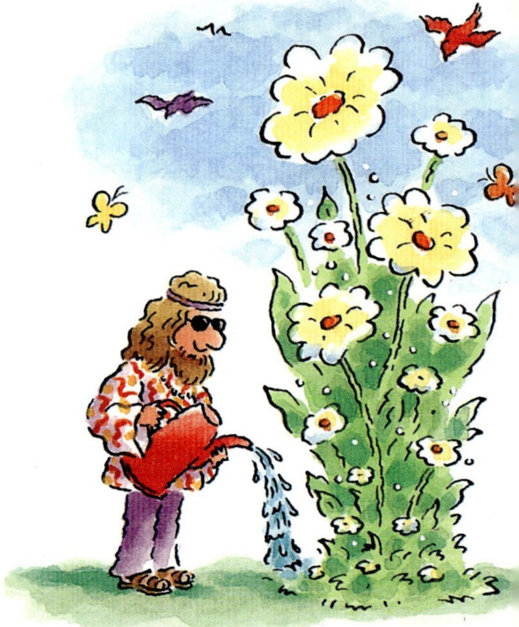

CAPRICORN: This teaming has all the thrills and sex appeal of two old socks. In separate drawers.

AQUARIUS: Laid-back, irresponsible Aquarius would bring about as much stability to your world as a volcanic eruption.

PISCES: You will adore Pisces until the first time the Fish shilly-shallies. And that will take about five minutes.

LEO: Lions eat Goats.

VIRGO: Strictly for masochists. Unfortunately, you qualify.

LIBRA: Libra loves a laugh. You laughed once—in 1982.

SCORPIO: The Scorpion loves, hates, stings, kisses wildly, but does everything with passion. The only thing you do with passion is try to figure out what that strange word means.

SAGITTARIUS: The best thing about Sagittarians is that they're never there to bug you.

COMPATIBILITY GUIDE
CAPRICORN AND...

ARIES: Aries is an exclamation point! You. Are. A. Period.

TAURUS: Your perfect mate. You can out-dull each other and see who dies of boredom first.

GEMINI: Twins were dancing on mountaintop; Goat kicked Twins and watched them drop.

CANCER: Cancer requires constant attention, but you're about as sensitive as a tire track.

CAPRICORN AT A GLANCE

Motto: What else do you want me to do?
Ruling planet: Down-to-earth
Element: Dishwater (as in dull as . . .)
Quality: Exciting as dirt
First desire: I don't really have any
Last desire: Figure out the first
Secret desire: Not to be asked so many questions
Animals: Earthworms
Key words: Dull and determined

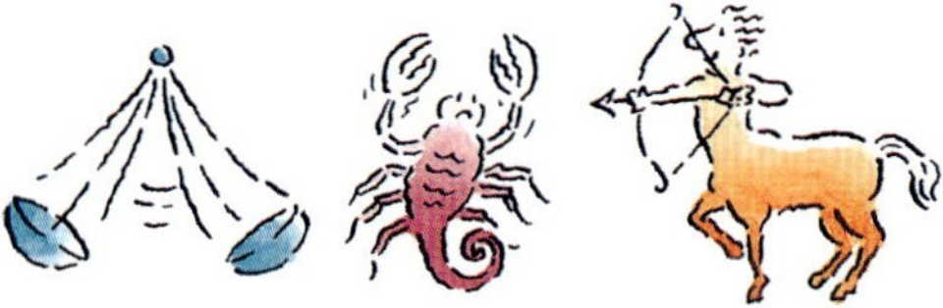

CAPRICORN the GOAT

DECEMBER 22– JANUARY 20

Sour Goat

Tough, stubborn, dour, and dutiful, the Goat is about as much fun as a shark attack.

Ever hear of kickin' back, kickin' out, kickin' up your heels? Nah—you're too busy doing the right thing. Here's a hint: Nobody cares about the right thing! People want to have fun! Boogie! Chill!

Your idea of a good time is contemplating your next disaster.

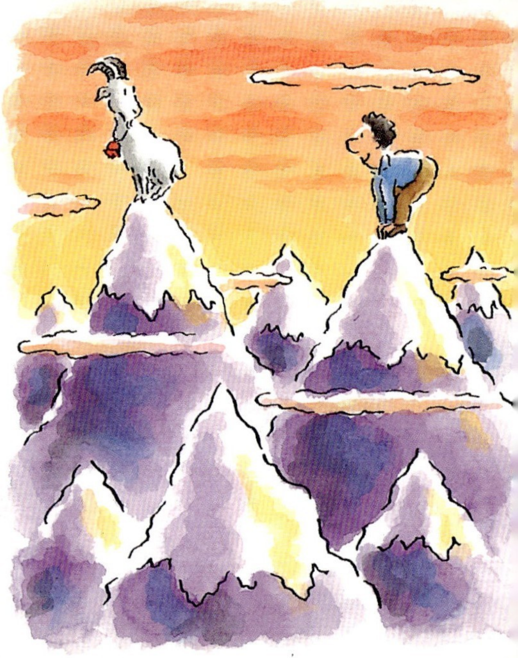

SAGITTARIUS: "Hi!" "Hi!" "Bye!" "Bye!"

CAPRICORN: Capricorn's idea of a good time is to stare at the walls for a while and brood.

AQUARIUS: You and this cool cucumber should hit it off. Unfortunately, your heads are so empty that you'll have nothing to say.

PISCES: This union will be tender, warm—and as stable as Jim Carrey on a bad day!

LEO: Stray once from the Lion's embrace, and you will become its next meal.

VIRGO: You might as well take up with a pair of talking handcuffs . . . that never stop criticizing you!

LIBRA: Libra methodically, judiciously weighs you, ponders, and finally makes a decision. By then, alas, you'll be under a tree in Zanzibar!

SCORPIO: To the Scorpion, you are merely a butterfly, which it would love to pin down. With its many legs.

COMPATIBILITY GUIDE
SAGITTARIUS AND . . .

ARIES: Fire meets flash fire, and all hell breaks loose!

TAURUS: By the time the Bull takes its first step out the door, you're halfway to the airport.

GEMINI: Quick, nervous, energetic, always on the move. You'll spend as much time together as pinballs . . . and with equal affection!

CANCER: Crab's response to trouble: Give me a hug! Your response to trouble: Give me the car keys!

SAGITTARIUS AT A GLANCE

Motto: Get me outta here!
Ruling planet: Any one you're not on now
Element: The air you fly through
Quality: Skittish
First desire: Leave
Last desire: Leave for good
Secret desire: Become the Fugitive!
Animals: Trains, planes, and Ferraris
Key words: Where, when, how do I get there?

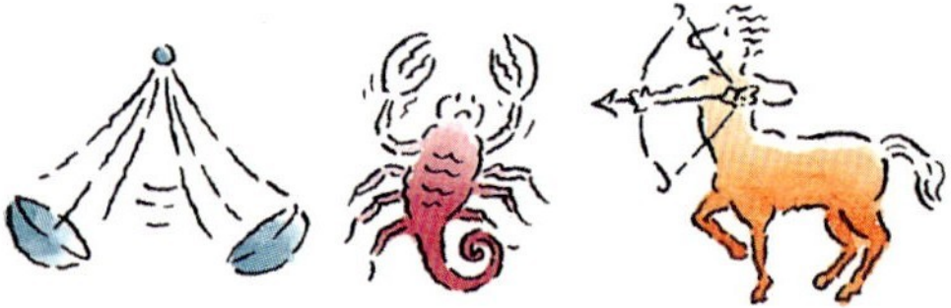

SAGITTARIUS the ARCHER

NOVEMBER 23 – DECEMBER 21
The Fast Track to Nowhere

They call you irresponsible. They call you unreliable. Throw in idiotic to boot!

The tiniest monkey wrench is thrown into the works, and what's your response? Get me out the door! You run away even when there's nothing to run from. An ocean wave has more direction than you do—and more backbone!

But there's always tomorrow . . . when you can catch another plane!

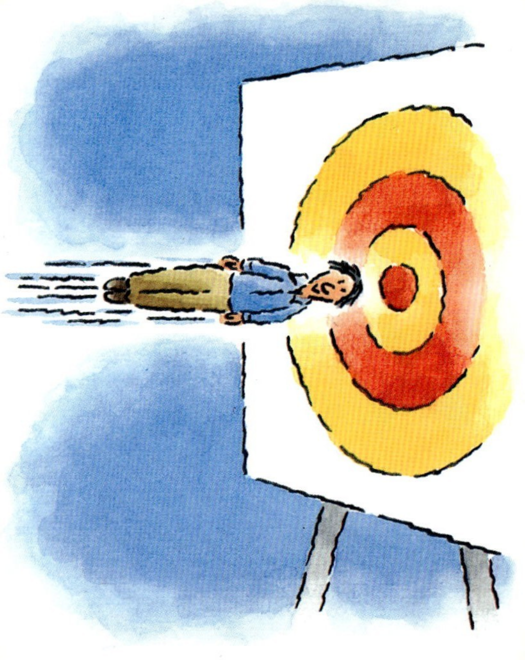

SAGITTARIUS: You demand fidelity. Sagittarius demands freedom. The Archer is pinned to the wall by the Scorpion's pincers.

CAPRICORN: The Goat represents grit, determination, responsibility. Can you imagine anything more boring?

AQUARIUS: A single night with this laid-back hippie will make you long for Capricorn.

PISCES: The Fish is sweet, loving, romantic—in short, the perfect victim!

death and destruction will lash all around. A good pairing otherwise.

LEO: Technically, you are not an insect, but the Lion doesn't like *anything* that crawls.

VIRGO: The Virgin's response to the world is to critique it. Your response to critics is to kill them.

LIBRA: Tolerant Libra can stand almost anyone—except you.

SCORPIO: Scorpio-meets-Cancer was hopscotch compared to *this* Armageddon. World War Three would be more peaceful!

COMPATIBILITY GUIDE
SCORPIO AND...

ARIES: The Ram would just as soon squash you as look at you.

TAURUS: Infinitely patient Taurus will be the ideal mate, until you go too far. Then the Bull will see red and charge.

GEMINI: Constant action and excitement! And when you get really ticked off, you'll have *two* of them to sting!

CANCER: Claws will snap, stingers will fly,

SCORPIO AT A GLANCE

Motto: I want it now!!!!!
Ruling planet: Out there
Element: Chaos
Quality: Raging
First desire: Kill it!
Last desire: Destroy it!
Secret desire: Total world domination
Animals: Venomous and disgusting
Key words: Crazy, nutso, whacked-out

SCORPIO the SCORPION

OCTOBER 24– NOVEMBER 22
The Scorpion Sting

You are a roller-coastering, manic-depressive nutcase!

Your rages are torrential! Your joys titanic! Your miseries cataclysmic! And you constantly scream at the top of your voice!

As subtle as a scorpion's sting! Willing to strike at the slightest provocation! A time bomb waiting to explode! With hardly a rational idea in your head.

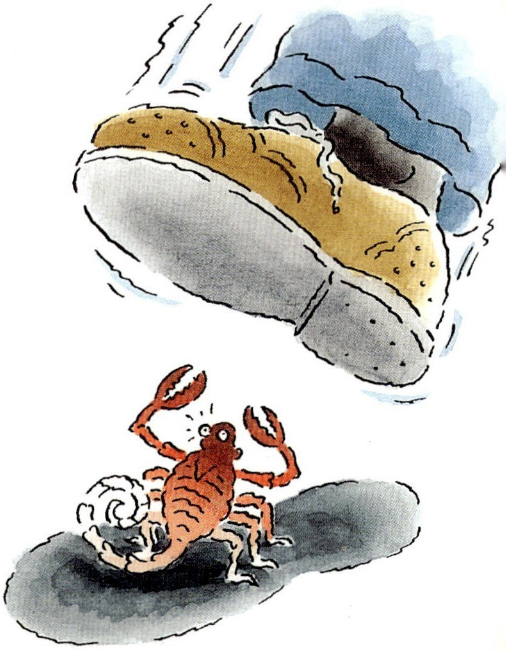

SCORPIO: Libra sees scorpion; *thinks*. Scorpion sees Libra; *stings*.

SAGITTARIUS: While you're trying to decide where to go, Sagittarius has been there and back. Maybe next time?

CAPRICORN: Capricorn always knows exactly what it wants. Unfortunately, it isn't you.

AQUARIUS: You know what happened when the mellow Aquarian met the undecided Libra? Nothing.

PISCES: Pisces swims in circles, Libra thinks in circles.

CANCER: Cancer wants to be reassured, but you'll have to think about it for a while.

LEO: What does the king of the jungle do with shilly-shallying namby-pambys? Throws them to the lions.

VIRGO: You never do much, so the Virgin won't have anything to criticize.

LIBRA: If wishy met washy it might be perfect— but you'll never come together because you'll both be uncertain of the time and place!

COMPATIBILITY GUIDE
LIBRA AND ...

ARIES: Aries attacks! You, on the other hand, might, might not.

TAURUS: What happens when the Bull gets really tired of your chronic indecision? Hoof-in-mouth disease for Libra.

GEMINI: You never know what you're thinking, and Gemini never knows what it's doing. These ships pass in the night out of sheer incompetence.

LIBRA AT A GLANCE

Motto: I'm really not *sure* . . .
Ruling planet: Indecision
Element: Fine and subtle confusion
Quality: Ambiguity
First desire: Not sure
Last desire: Can't say
Secret desire: Isn't clear
Animals: Haven't decided yet
Key words: Let's not rush into anything

LIBRA the SCALES

SEPTEMBER 24– OCTOBER 23
All Talk and No Walk

Can't make up your mind? Can see all ten sides of a coin, even though it only has two sides? Can think of a thousand reasons not to do something? Can sit on the fence until you become the fence? Can't ever make a statement because you're always asking a question?

This is your life, Libra.

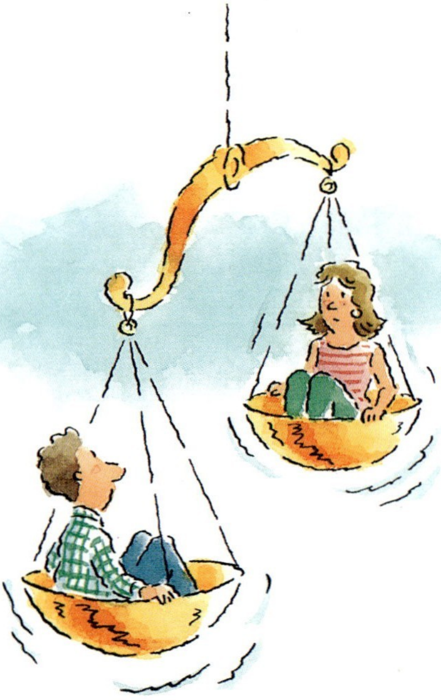

SAGITTARIUS: So long as there are windows and doors, the Archer will avoid your nit-picking.

CAPRICORN: You're depressing and Capricorn is depressed. Hand grenade meets pipe bomb.

AQUARIUS: Mellow Aquarius will agree with everything you say. This will give you nothing to complain about, and what's the fun of that?

PISCES: Sweet-tempered Pisces is easy prey—but be prepared for a thousand floods of tears.

LEO: Order a cat around and it'll walk snootily away. Order a Lion around and it'll tear off your head.

VIRGO: What's the point of living if you have no one to criticize?

LIBRA: Libra is so balanced that you can pick on it *forever* and still have someone to talk to about how unappreciated you are.

SCORPIO: You know what that stinger is for? To silence critics.

COMPATIBILITY GUIDE
VIRGO AND...

ARIES: The warrior slob comes home and receives a lecture and an order to clean up? I don't think so.

TAURUS: The Bull will take your bossing for years. Until one day Taurus obliterates the china shop...

GEMINI: Chaotic and irresponsible, the Twins will be in double misery until the day you die.

CANCER: Pincers squeeze hard when the Crab doesn't get its tender lovin'.

VIRGO AT A GLANCE

Motto: I just cleaned that!
Ruling planet: Whichever one is in perfect position at the time
Element: Priggishness
Quality: Priggish
First desire: To be a prig
Last desire: To be a perfect prig
Secret desire: To be loved for the prig that you really are!
Animals: Those without feathers, hair, or anything that's dirty
Key words: Clean your room! Now!

VIRGO the VIRGIN

AUGUST 24–SEPTEMBER 23
Virgin Priss

You dot every *i*. You cross every *t*. You put every paper clip in its allotted place, which is, of course, meticulously clean. You are a crashing bore!

And you know what else? You lecture. You're superior. You're always right. And you always let everyone know about it. So why does anyone like you?

They don't!

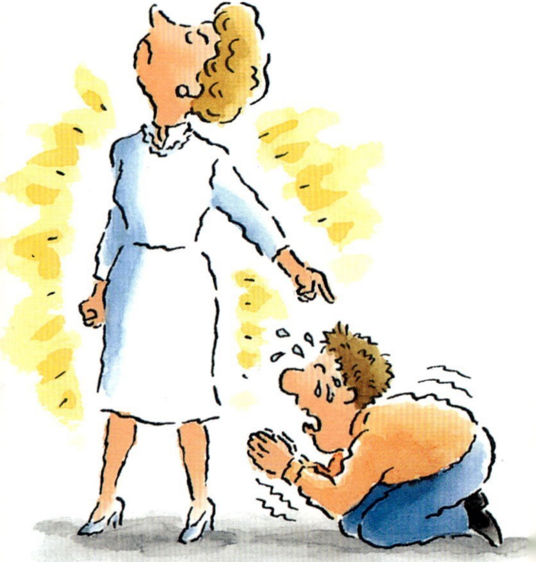

SCORPIO: Scorpion tells truth. Scorpion stings Lion. Scorpion crushed on rock.

SAGITTARIUS: Archer shoots arrow into the sky. Arrow hits Lion. Archer must die.

CAPRICORN: The last thing this depressing sign wants to hear about is how great *you* are. Old tires would be more appreciative.

AQUARIUS: Uh—no.

PISCES: The Fish is so loving it can even put up with *you*. May Pisces rest in peace.

CANCER: Cancer wants to be noticed. With you around? Ha!

LEO: Ever see two lions duking it out because both thought their manes were the most splendid in creation? When this battle is over there will be enough cat food left to last for the next six months.

VIRGO: Kind Virgins are good for the Lion to eat.

LIBRA: Calm, judicious, dignified—and able to see through all your boasting. Forget about it!

COMPATIBILITY GUIDE
LEO AND...

ARIES: You both think you're the greatest, so sparks will constantly fly—and a little blood may flow.

TAURUS: Far too grown-up for your fantastic self-love.

GEMINI: Drawn to the superficial and showy, always running off at the mouth: If the Twins only talked about *you* all the time, this would be bliss! Alas, they won't.

LEO AT A GLANCE

Motto: Aren't I fantastic!!!!!
Ruling planet: The Sun
Element: Hot air
Quality: *Unbelievably* conceited
First desire: To be loved
Last desire: To be admired
Secret desire: To be worshiped!
Animals: All things bright and beautiful
Key words: Me, me, me

LEO the LION

JULY 24–AUGUST 23

The Lion's Roar

You know why you need a mane? Because it makes your head look smaller than the balloon it really is!

And we're not talking about party balloons here—it's a hot-air balloon.

Lawyers are liars, politicians are thieves, and Leos are conceited. These are the three laws of the jungle of which you *believe* you are king! Underneath you're just an overstuffed cat.

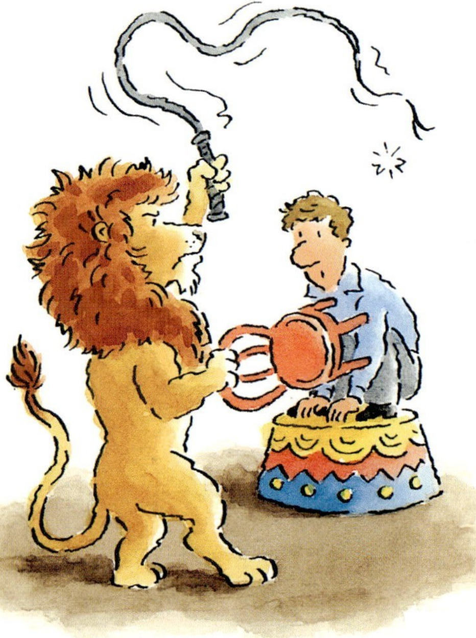

SAGITTARIUS: Use your pincer to wave bye-bye, because the Archer is permanently out the door.

CAPRICORN: About as sensitive as a tennis shoe.

AQUARIUS: This mellow reformer will actually make you long for Scorpio's poison!

PISCES: Both are sweet, tender, caring, sensitive. And when you get angry, remember: Fish are good to eat!

LEO: Lions like Crabs. A good-sized one fits nicely into Leo's mouth!

VIRGO: You are warm and demanding. Virgo is cold and demanding. A lose-lose proposition.

LIBRA: The only thing these Scales are good for is weighing how much crabmeat lurks beneath your shell.

SCORPIO: Scorpio's tempestuous stinger can pierce right through your tough covering, but at least this will *really* give you something to cry about!

COMPATIBILITY GUIDE
CANCER AND...

ARIES: Warlike Aries will destroy you in a nanosecond.

TAURUS: The Bull can deal with your sensitivity, up to a point. Then it's crab cocktail time!

GEMINI: You want a shoulder to cry on, but the Twins are never there.

CANCER: Beneath that tough shell lies a total wimp. You think another Crab will care about *your* problems?

CANCER AT A GLANCE

Motto: I weep, therefore I am!
Ruling planet: The weepy Moon
Element: Water (as in tears)
Quality: Crabby
First desire: Be sensitive
Last desire: Pretend to be even more sensitive!
Secret desire: To die a martyr
Animals: Those with protective shells
Key words: Waah! Boo hoo!

CANCER the CRAB

JUNE 22–JULY 23
The Crabby Crab

You think it's a joke that people call you the crab? Hey, it's a *compliment!* You should hear the other things they say! Such as:

"I'm so sick of that oversensitivity!"

"Look sideways and the Crab starts to cry!"

"Why be so prickly all the time if you're such a baby underneath?"

But cheer up! Otherwise, you'll start to weep.

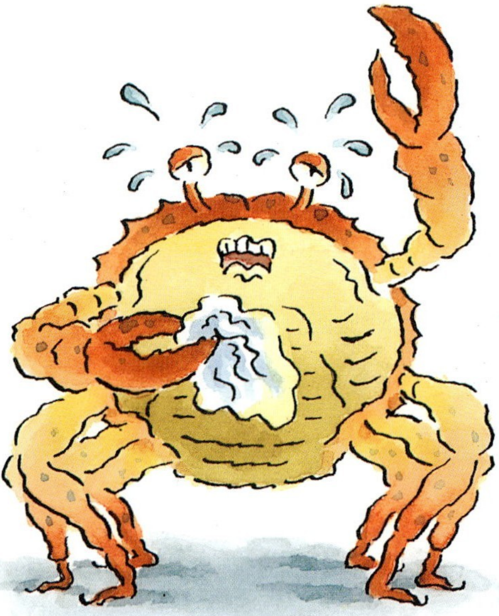

SAGITTARIUS: If the Twins had a twin, it would be Sagittarius. But the two of you are too busy crossing the globe to ever meet, so how can you have a relationship?

CAPRICORN: Capricorn is dead serious, but the two words are the same as far as you're concerned.

AQUARIUS: Hippie meets dippy, and the relationship is drippy.

PISCES: Pisces has needs, so you need to get outta there!

LEO: Talk about the Lion's greatness day and night and you will shine. Talk about anything else and Leo will claw you.

VIRGO = control. Gemini = chaos. This partnership = 0.

LIBRA: When you're not too busy wandering, and Libra's not too busy flirting, this will be a perfect union.

SCORPIO: Jealous, combative Scorpio meets flighty, flirtatious Gemini? Not unless you have an antidote for that stinger.

COMPATIBILITY GUIDE
GEMINI AND...

ARIES: No way.

TAURUS: Glib Gemini can talk its way out of almost anything, but not when cornered by a fed-up Bull. Forget about this pairing—value your life.

GEMINI: What happens when two incredibly hyper people get together and hyper each other out? They die of exhaustion.

CANCER: Gemini flitters and Cancer retreats into its shell. Hasta la vista, baby.

GEMINI AT A GLANCE

Motto: Get me outta here fast!
Ruling planet: Mercury
Element: Air
Quality: Nervous
First desire: Talk
Last desire: Leave
Secret desire: Find a place to settle down and then blow it up
Animals: Hummingbirds, water spiders, anything that scoots
Key words: Profoundly superficial

GEMINI the TWINS

MAY 22 – JUNE 21
The Two-Faced Twins

Description of a Gemini: duplicitous, two-faced, talking out both sides of the mouth, speaking with forked tongue, split personality, wolf in sheep's clothing, nutso. Sound good thus far?

Then try: fast, nervous, skittish, high metabolism, obsessive talker, irresponsible, unreliable, restless.

Hint: This is not the portrait of a stable person.

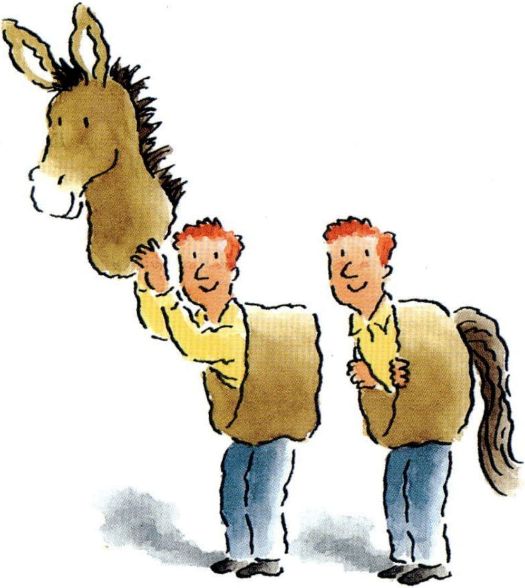

SAGITTARIUS: This self-absorbed free spirit will last about as long as a toreador in red.

CAPRICORN: Pleasant. Comfy. No sparks.

AQUARIUS: Aquarius wants the world to be full of peace and love. Yuck.

PISCES: Sensual, like you, but ultra, ultrasensitive. Bellow too loudly and the Fish will dive back into the sea.

but you may want to kick the Crab into the ocean when it keeps weeping for no reason.

LEO: Lion preens. Lion boasts. Bull gores Lion.

VIRGO: Virgin complains. Virgin gives orders. Bull gores Virgin.

LIBRA: A wonderful sign, but a frightful flirt. The Bull does not look lightly upon flirtation.

SCORPIO: A prickly, tempestuous sign that could lead you to bliss. If not, you can simply crush it with your hoof.

COMPATIBILITY GUIDE
TAURUS AND...

ARIES: Aries is constantly on the move, and you are constantly on the couch.

TAURUS: A marriage made in Heaven, except that neither of you will ever leave the house—or even the bedroom—and will have pizza delivered until you burst.

GEMINI: Flashy Gemini will talk, talk, talk until you put your hoof in its mouth.

CANCER: Cancer's moodiness won't bother you,

TAURUS AT A GLANCE

Motto: I'll do it tomorrow
Ruling planet: Venus, the goddess of love
Element: Sleep
Quality: Self-indulgent and lazy
First desire: Have fun
Last desire: Sleep
Secret desire: Have so much fun I *fall* asleep
Animal: Bull
Key words: The living-room sofa

TAURUS the BULL

APRIL 21– MAY 21
Lazy Taurus

Bulls are slow, patient, and famed for their stubbornness, but that is only the surface you. The real Taurus is incredibly lazy and loves to wallow in sensual indulgence.

The lawn needs to be cut? Hey, I'm watching TV! That legal brief needs to be filed? Not now, I just took off my shoes. Tomorrow is another day—and with any luck, you'll sleep through it.

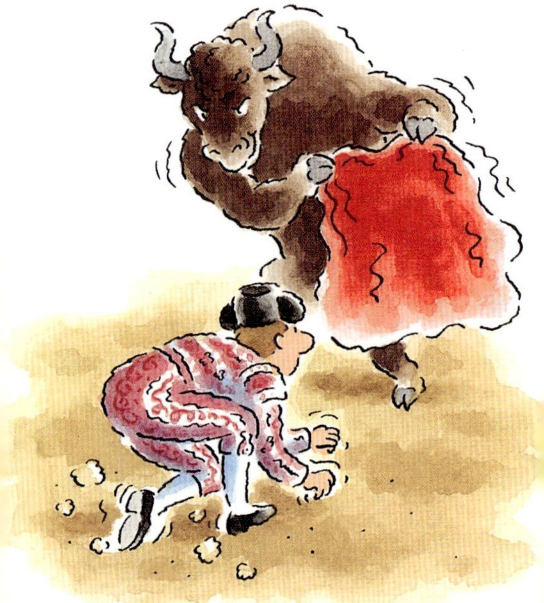

SAGITTARIUS: Push the Archer just one step too far and Sagittarius will be out the door in no time.

CAPRICORN: Cautious Capricorn will bore you to death.

AQUARIUS: Mellow Aquarius can get along with just about anyone, and this will *really* make you mad.

PISCES: Pliant Pisces will do whatever you want half the time . . . and spend the other half crying over your insensitivity.

dling, but you're about as delicate as a hydrogen bomb.

LEO: Leo's monumental arrogance is as ferocious as your ferocity, but will the splendid Lion care about a nutcase like you?

VIRGO: Virgo constantly criticizes; your response to criticism is to tie on the boxing gloves.

LIBRA: Calm, judicious Libra can stand a lot—but can't stand you.

SCORPIO: Scorpio is all smothering affection one day and bristling sting the next. You're sort of the same way, only without the affection.

COMPATIBILITY GUIDE
ARIES AND . . .

ARIES: Fire meets fire, creating more fire and possibly destroying the world (or at least the house).

TAURUS: The Bull is calm, slow, and trusting. Get out of line, however, and Taurus *will* gore you. You make the call.

GEMINI: Witty Gemini will make one wisecrack too many one day and wind up in the hospital.

CANCER: The moody Crab requires delicate han-

ARIES AT A GLANCE

Motto: I crush, therefore I am
Ruling planet: Mars, the god of war
Element: Combustion
Quality: Explosive
First desire: Crush them
Last desire: Slush them
Secret desire: Mush them
Animals: Ram, rhinoceros, anything horned that likes to attack
Key words: Headstrong, impulsive, mean

ARIES the RAM

MARCH 21– APRIL 20
Head-Busting Aries

Aries is the first sign of the zodiac and a leader in all things. Blazing trails and smashing heads is what you do best.

Rams are warlike, impulsive bullies, quick to take offense and even quicker to break someone's jaw. You know the guy who blew up the house to kill a mouse? That's you.

P.S. The mouse is still around.

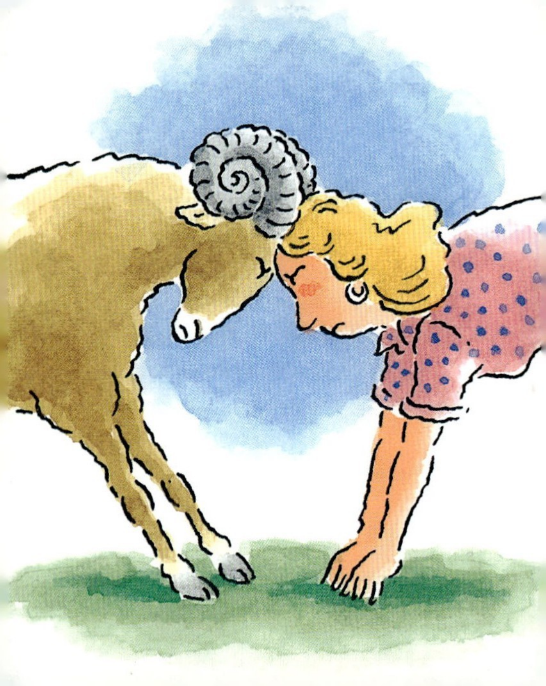

thing. In fact, they mean twelve things, which are called sun signs. This means the Sun was shining when you were born.

It also means that you're a Pisces or Leo, depending on when you were born. We'll explain later.

After that, the meaning of your life should be pretty clear.

INTRODUCTION

Astrology predates recorded history and possibly recorded thought. Ever since early Man and Woman looked up to the sky and saw that something was there, they've been trying to figure out what it was.

Now, through the miracle of technology, we know: planets and stars.

But those planets and stars are not merely planets and stars: They mean some-

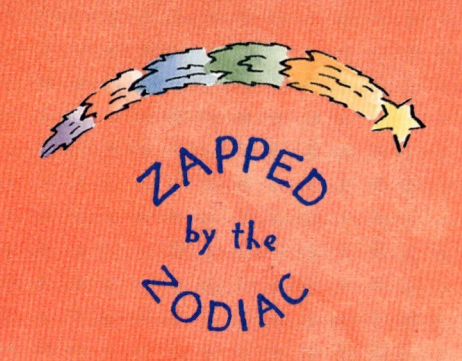

ZAPPED by the ZODIAC

*Zapped by the Zodiac:
The Cynic's Astrology Guide*
Copyright © 1998 by Armand Eisen. All rights reserved. Printed in Hong Kong. No part of this book may be used or reproduced in any manner whatsoever without written permission except in the case of reprints in the context of reviews. For information write Andrews McMeel Publishing, an Andrews McMeel Universal company, 4520 Main Street, Kansas City, Missouri 64111.

www.andrewsmcmeel.com

ISBN: 0-8362-3598-3

Library of Congress Catalog
Card Number: 97-74535

ZAPPED by the ZODIAC
The Cynic's Astrology Guide

Amadeo Zorro Aster

Illustrated by Larry Ross

Ariel Books

Andrews McMeel Publishing

Kansas City

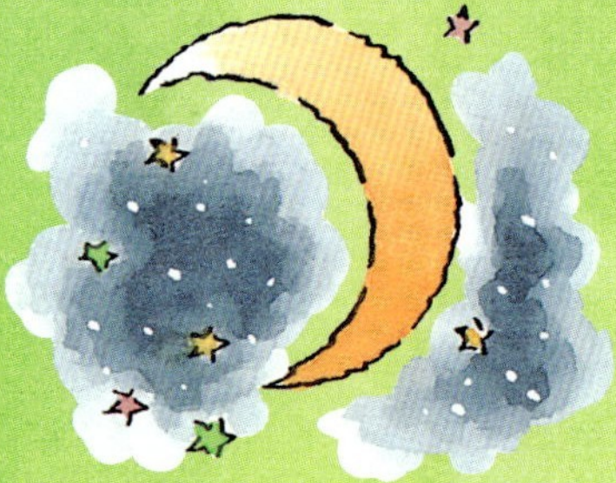

ZAPPED by the ZODIAC